For those whose lives were cut short everywhere,
including Bialystok June 27, 1941.
Your memory is a blessing. Love lives on.
— N.C.

To my parents.
— Y.N.

Text copyright © 2019 Nancy Churnin
Illustrations copyright © 2019 Yevgenia Nayberg
Book design by Simon Stahl

CIP data for this book is available from the Library of Congress.

Published by Creston Books, LLC
www.crestonbooks.co

Printed and bound in China
5 4 3 2 1

Martin & Anne

The Kindred Spirits of
Dr. Martin Luther King, Jr. and Anne Frank

By Nancy Churnin

Illustrated by
Yevgenia Nayberg

Creston Books

In 1929, two babies were born on opposite sides of the ocean. They never met. They didn't even speak the same language. But their hearts beat with the same hope.

On January 15, Martin's father, mother, and older sister beamed at their beautiful baby in Atlanta, Georgia.

On June 12, Anne's father, mother, and older sister cooed at their beautiful baby in Frankfurt, Germany.

But not everyone thought Martin and Anne were beautiful. When Martin was old enough to go to school, he had to go to a different one than his best friend because his skin was dark. Even worse, his friend stopped playing with him. Martin's skin hadn't changed. But suddenly, his friend cared when he hadn't before. That made no sense!

When Anne was ready for school, Adolf Hitler, the leader of the Nazi party, was elected to lead Germany. Jewish children like Anne were no longer allowed in public schools. Anne's family fled Germany for Holland, but when Hitler invaded Holland, anti-Jewish laws followed. Anne's school closed its doors to her. Suddenly, her friends didn't want to play with her anymore.

Everywhere Martin went, he saw signs that said "Whites Only." He wasn't welcome in public parks, swimming pools, or restaurants. Martin didn't think that was fair.

Everywhere Anne went, she had to wear a yellow Star of David that let people know she was Jewish. She couldn't buy ice cream or go to a movie. Every day, more signs blared, "No Jews Allowed." Her father couldn't sell to non-Jewish customers. Nazis burned books by Jewish authors.

When Martin was 13, he won a speech competition, talking about black and white children playing together in harmony. He wondered if the right words could one day change unfair laws.

When Anne was 13, she got a diary for her birthday. She was happy she could share her most private thoughts with Kitty, the name she gave her journal. But soon after she began writing, Jews were rounded up and sent to death camps. Anne and her family hid in the attic over her father's business. They had to be very quiet. They couldn't go outside. Trapped in the attic, Anne described how beautiful the world outside was, how light could brighten the deepest darkness.

Martin finished high school at 15. Most colleges were for whites only, so he went to Morehouse College, a school for black students. There he learned about the Indian leader Mahatma Gandhi and how he won rights for his people using peaceful protests. Could the same thing work in America? Martin decided to become a minister who would lead his people to stand up for justice.

Anne, hidden in the attic, continued her studies as best she could. And every day, she wrote in her diary about her dreams for a better world. Even with all the hate around her, Anne believed that people were really good at heart.

When Rosa Parks was arrested for refusing to give up her bus seat to a white man, Martin, now a minister, organized protest marches. He gave speeches. He told people not to ride the buses until everyone was treated fairly.

Martin shared his dream of a world where all were truly considered equal.
His words gave people courage and strength.

While Martin grew older, Anne's 15th year was her last. The Nazis stormed Anne's hiding place. They arrested her family and the friends hiding with them. Anne's diary was left behind, pages scattering on the floor of the dusty attic.

But she still believed in the power of simple acts of kindness.

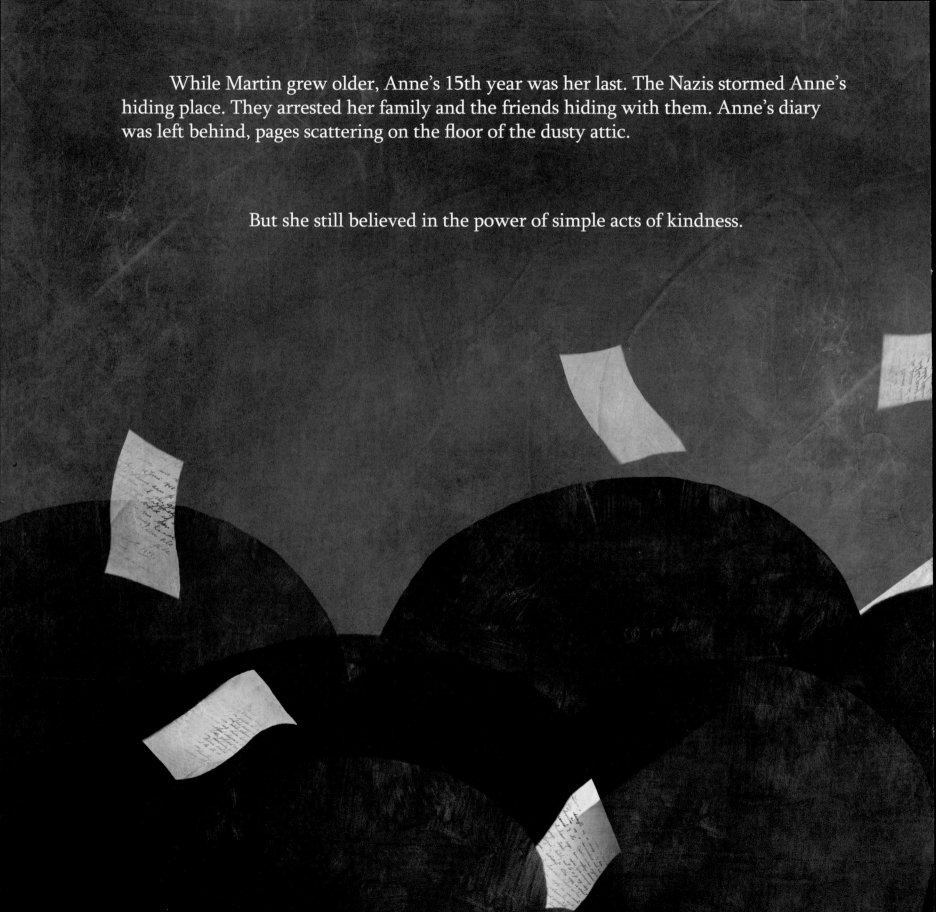

Martin won the Nobel Peace Prize when he was 35. He worked with President Lyndon Johnson to help pass the Civil Rights Act of 1964. At last, those ugly "Whites Only" signs were against the law.

Only a few weeks before the concentration camp was liberated, Anne died, along with her older sister.

She would have been amazed that her diary, rescued by a family friend, became a best-seller. Her father, the only one in her family to survive the camps, had her book published. Actors performed her words on stage and film. The cramped rooms where she hid in Amsterdam became a museum dedicated to speaking out against hate.

When Martin was 39, he was shot and killed by a man who didn't believe black people deserved the same rights as white people. But no one could kill the way Martin inspired others.

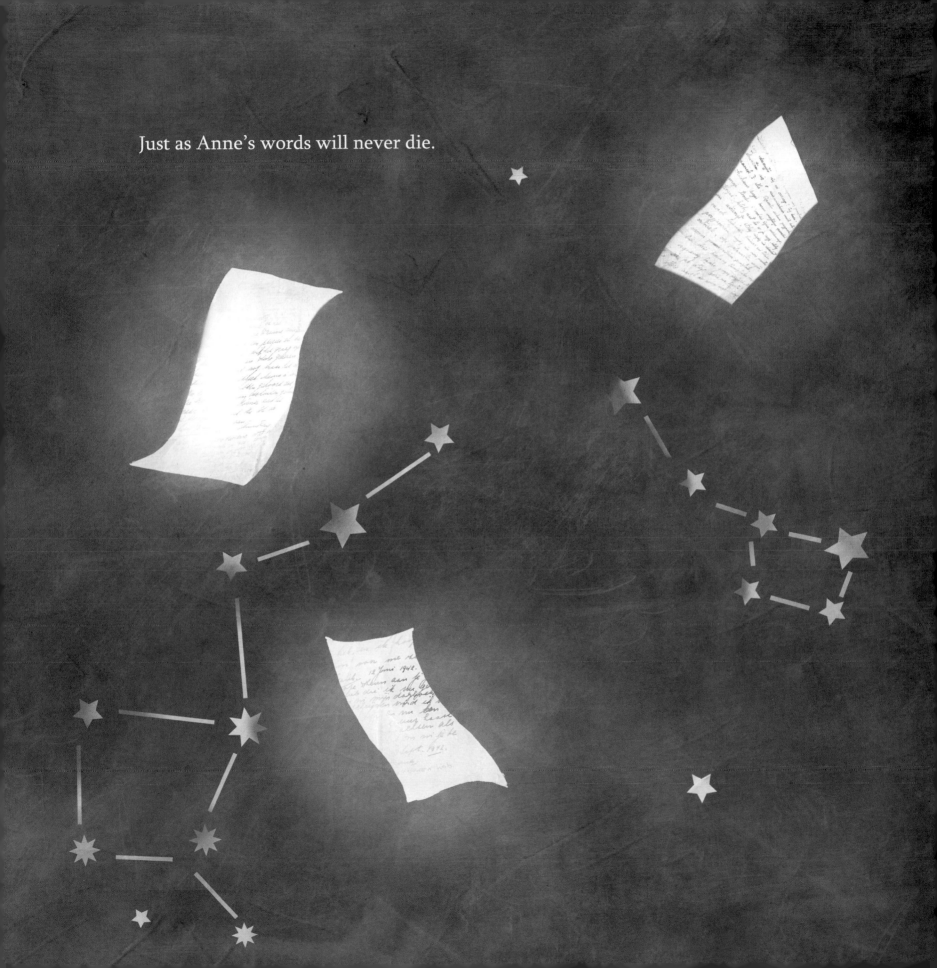

Just as Anne's words will never die.

Martin and Anne were born in different places, but they both dreamed that one day all babies would be seen as beautiful. As all babies are.

Love is stronger than hate.

Kindness can heal the world.

Timeline

1929:   Martin Luther King, Jr. is born in Atlanta, Georgia on January 15.

1929:   Anne Frank is born in Frankfurt am Main, Germany on June 12.

1933:   Adolph Hitler is named Chancellor of Germany, the head of the government.

1934:   Anne's family moves to Amsterdam, fleeing anti-Jewish laws in Germany.

1939:   Hitler's armies invade Poland. In response, France and Britain declare war on Germany. World War II begins.

1942:   Anne starts writing in her diary and keeps writing when her family goes into hiding in the attic above her father's business.

1944:   The Nazis discover Anne and her family. They are sent to concentration camps where Jews are systematically murdered in gas chambers, shot, or worked to death.

1945:   Anne and her sister, Margot, die of typhus at the Bergen-Belsen camp in March. The camp is liberated weeks later in April, 1945. Of the 107,000 Jews deported from the Netherlands, only 5,000 survived. More than 1.5 million Jewish children and 6 million European Jews were murdered by the Nazis between 1933 and 1945.

1947:   Martin is ordained a minister.

1929–1950:   The Equal Justice Initiative gives a figure of 202 African Americans being lynched between 1929 and 1950.

1952:   Anne's diary, called *Anne Frank: The Diary of a Young Girl,* is published in English.

1955:   The play, *The Diary of Anne Frank,* by Frances Goodrich and Albert Hackett, wins the Pulitzer Prize for Drama.

1955–1956:   Martin starts a boycott of buses in Montgomery, Alabama that leads to everyone being able to sit where they want.

1957:   The Anne Frank Foundation is established to maintain the Anne Frank House in Amsterdam and to advocate against anti-Semitism and racism.

1963:   Martin leads the March on Washington and gives a speech about equality called "I Have a Dream" on the steps of the Lincoln Memorial.

1964:   Martin is awarded the Nobel Peace Prize.

1968:   Martin is assassinated on April 4 in a hotel room in Memphis, Tennessee.

1968:   Two months after Martin's death, James Earl Ray, a fugitive from prison, is arrested and charged with Martin's murder. He is sentenced to 99 years and dies in prison.

1986:   Martin Luther King Jr. Day becomes a national holiday observed on or near Martin's birthday of January 15.

Selected Bibliography

Adler, David A. *A Picture Book of Martin Luther King, Jr.* New York: Holiday House, 1989.

Carson, Clayborne (editor). *The Autobiography of Martin Luther King, Jr.* New York: Warner Books, 1998.

Jakoubek, Robert. *Martin Luther King, Jr.: Civil Rights Leader.* New York: Chelsea House Publishers, 2005.

Kennon, Caroline. *Anne Frank in Her Own Words.* New York: Gareth Stevens Publishing, 2014.

McDonough, Yona Zeldis. *Anne Frank.* New York: Henry Holt & Company, 1997.

Metselaar, Menno and Van der Rol, Ruud. *Anne Frank: Her Life in Words and Pictures.* New York: Flash Point, 2009.

About the Authors

Nancy Churnin is the theater critic for the *Dallas Morning News* by day, children's book writer by night. *Manjhi Moves a Mountain,* her first book with Creston, won the South Asia Book Award, was a Junior Library Guild Selection, a Eureka Honor Book, an Ezra Jack Keats Award Finalist, a Children's & Teen Choice Book Awards Finalist, an ILA–CBC Children's Choices, an NCSS–CBC Notable Social Studies Selection 2018, and a North Texas Book Awards Finalist.

Yevgenia Nayberg is painter, illustrator, and stage designer. A native of Kiev, Ukraine, she graduated from The National School of Arts. Yevgenia's paintings have been featured in solo exhibitions in New York City, Miami, Los Angeles, and Moscow as well as in numerous international group art shows. She has designed sets and costumes for over 40 theatrical productions and received a number of prestigious awards for her stage designs. Her illustrations have appeared in children's books and magazines as well as on album covers, book covers and theatre posters. Yevgenia lives in New York City.

"This story brilliantly connects two amazing humans by their birth year and by sharing their stories of finding hope in unimaginably dark circumstances. A poignant read for parents and teachers who want their children to build empathy and appreciate how we are all connected, while being full of important history."
—Naomi Chamblin, Napa Bookmine

"A wonderful weaving of the stories of two amazing and courageous people who both answer hatred with love."
—Kristen Carvalho, Board Member, Anne Frank House, Inc of Washington, DC.

"A poignant narrative paralleling the lives of two well known figures in history who aspire for peace and freedom, all while reminding the reader of the power of the written and spoken word."
—Meghan Hennick, 3rd grade teacher, Walworth Barbour American International School